SPIRITISM 101

Luis Hu Rivas

Understanding Spiritism in only few minutes
Spiritism 101

1st English Edition
September 2016
© 2016 USSF – J. Korngold

ISBN 978-0985279370
LCCN 2016949221

Contact: info@spiritist.us
www.spiritist.us

Cover Design
Luis Hu Rivas

Book Design
Luis Hu Rivas

English Translation
Jussara Korngold

Library of Congress Cataloging-in-Publication Data
Hu Rivas, Luis
Spiritism 101 / Luis Hu Rivas
translated by USSF – New York, NY: United States Spiritist Federation, 2016.
Original title: Espiritismo Fácil
1. Spirituality. 2. Spiritism. 3. Christianity. 4. Philosophy

UNITED STATES
SPIRITIST FEDERATION

Content

Spiritist Principle

Spiritism is expressed in three aspects: science, philosophy and religion. The fundamental principles lie in the restoration of the Gospel of Jesus, in order to renew humankind and it's spiritual future.

Precedents

The Hydesville phenomena
The turning tables
The work of Allan Kardec

SPIRITISM

Science that observes and studies the spirits. From its communications and its teachings, arises a philosophy that leads to moral, religious and spiritual transformation in human beings.

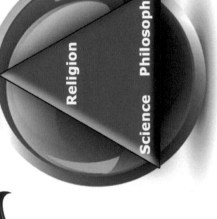

IMMORTALITY OF THE SOUL

The existence of spirits has no end.

Perispirit

Semi-material body that connects the soul to the physical body.

Spirit

Intelligent being of the divine creation.

GOD

Supreme Intelligence, first cause of all things.

Moral laws

Ten laws resulting from the natural law, which is the Law of God.

Elements of the Universe

Spirit and matter. And above all, God.

Spiritual influence
Spirits influence us more than we imagine, driving us in general.

MEDIUMSHIP
Everyone who feels the influence of spirits is a medium.

Free will
Human beings have freedom to think and to

Evolution
Spirits evolve to higher levels.

Progress

REINCARNATION
Spirits go through many successive existences until their purification.

Action of Spirits in Nature
Spirits are instruments of God and influence Nature.

INHABITED WORLD
All the planets in the universe are inhabited.

Spirit world
At the time of death, the soul returns to the spiritual world.

Cause and effect
Divine law that governs all actions of spirits.

Divine Justice

Base: JESUS' GOSPEL
Jesus is the guide and the most perfect model for humans.

The Three Revelations

There are, in Europe and America, three great Spirituals revelations. The first, Moses with the Ten Commandments; the second, Jesus with the Gospel; and the third, Spiritism, the world of the Spirits, life after death and the immortality of the soul.

Will Spiritism mark a new era? Without a doubt. When humanity gets to know Spiritism it will understand that life goes on, that it is useless to remain attached to material things, and that it is worth to practice good.

Will Science and Religion walk hand in hand one day? Yes, when both know the teachings of Spiritism they will find out that the soul exists, that there is a real invisible world, and there are Divine Laws in action. They will both change their radical thoughts, science will become spiritual and religion will use reason.

1st Revelation – Moses

Moses received the first spiritual revelation in the Ten Commandments. This happened 1250 years before Christ.

The Ten Commandments

I. I am the Lord, your God.
II. Thou shall bring no false idols before me.
III. Do not take the name of the Lord in vain.
IV. Remember the Sabbath and keep it holy.
V. Honor thy father and thy mother.
VI. Thou shall not kill.
VII. Thou shall not commit adultery.
VIII. Thou shall not steal.
IX. Thou shall not bear false witness against your neighbor.
X. Thou shall not covet your neighbor's wife (or anything that belongs to your neighbor).

2nd Revelation – Jesus

Jesus reveals to us the law of unconditional love when he says: "love God above all things and your neighbor as yourself", and he tells us the importance to do good in the Beatitudes.

Beatitudes

1. Blessed are the poor in spirit,
2. Blessed are those who mourn,
3. Blessed are the meek,
4. Blessed are those who hunger and thirst for righteousness,
5. Blessed are the merciful,
6. Blessed are the pure in heart,
7. Blessed are the peacemakers,
8. Blessed are those who are persecuted because of righteousness,
9. Blessed are you when people insult you, persecute you and falsely say all kinds of evil against you because of me.

Is Spiritism the Promised Consoler?

Spiritism is the consoler promised by Jesus two thousand years ago. Spiritism came to explain to us, why we are living in this world, and what will be our future.

At the time of Jesus, it was not possible to people to understand this knowledge.

The first revelation came from Moses, the second came from Jesus with the Gospel, but the third one did not come with a person (Allan Kardec), but rather from a group of Spirits that brought it to us.

Name:
Three revelations of the West
Dates: 1250 BCE
Moses 1250 BCE
Jesus 0-33 CE
Spiritism (1857 -)
Concept: from Latin,
To reveal, whose source, means revelare, veil, literally means the velum, veil, beneath the to get out and, figuratively, veil—and, figuratively, unveil.

3rd Revelation – Spiritism

It comes to reveal that we are Immortal Spirits, and that death does not exist. All that Jesus and Moses stated is real. Those who practice love and goodness will be rewarded in the spirit realm.

Spiritist Principles

1. Existence of God
2. Immortality of the Soul
3. Reincarnation
4. Inhabited Worlds
5. Mediumship
6. Law of Cause and Effect
7. Free-Will
8. Spiritual Influence
9. Evolution
10. The cornerstone: The Gospel of Jesus

The Hydesville Phenomena

In a small village in the United States, called Hydesville, a series of paranormal phenomena happened drawing much attention.
It was the year of 1848, at the house where the Fox family was living. A certain night, noises and rappings were heard on the walls from everywhere. Overcome by fear the Fox's girls could not sleep and went to their parent's room, but the noises continued.
Frightened, one of the girls had the idea to clap to communicate, establishing one clap for "yes" and two claps for "no". They found out that a Spirit was making the noises, and he said that he was a salesperson who was murdered in that same house years ago by the older owners. The girls gained fame with the incident and repeated the phenomenon in several places in America.

Who was the Spirit?

He was a peddler named Charles Rosma. Before the house was sold to the Fox family, the tenant that lived there murdered Rosma. The corpse was hidden in a false wall.

Name:
The Hydesville Phenomena
Date:
March 31st, 1848
Category:
Physical phenomena manifestation
Description:
Rappings or noises
Relevance:
This occurrence is the starting point of Spiritism.

House of the Fox family where in March 31st, 1848 the noises were heard.

Image of the Fox sisters, 1850, from left to right Margaret, Katherine and Leah Fox.

Image that represents the Spirits approaching the house of the Fox family.

Who was the Fox family?

It was a family consisting of father, mother and three daughters, called Margaret, 14, and Kate, 11. Leah, the oldest, lived in Rochester. They were Methodists and because of that they initially believed that the raps were produced by the "devil" and not a spirit.

Hydesville is located in the United States, in the State of New York.

Fonte: Google

The precise location is in Wayne County, distant about 19 miles from the city of Rochester.

Font: Google

How did the Spirits speak?

At first they communicated through rappings, one for "yes" and two for "no". Afterwards an alphabet was created in which each letter would correspond to a certain number of raps. One for A, two for B, three for C, and so on.

This illustration shows the parent's room when the raps started and Kate received answers for her signals.

The Hydesville Phenomena

Because of the importance of these phenomena and the curiosity of people, the Fox family had to move to New York City in order to continue with the public meetings.

The Turning Tables

The phenomenon called "Turning Tables" was practiced with three legs tables and people put their hands on their surface or stood around the table waiting for them to move.

At the time the phenomenon was seen as a form of entertainment during meetings of the high society in Europe, mainly in France. We're talking of a phenomenon that occurred between the years 1850-1855, when they caught the attention of a French pedagogue who would later be known as Allan Kardec. He studied the movements produced by the table and found out that they were caused by spirits.

How were the tables made?

They were simple. They had a base and three legs. The interesting thing was that the tables not only stood in one leg to answer questions, but also moved in all directions, they turned on the fingers of the participants and sometimes they even rose up in the air.

Name:
Turning tables
Date:
1850-1855
Location:
Europe
Category:
Physical Effect Phenomena
Relevance:
The turning tables represent the starting point of Spiritism in Europe.

Participants
Several members of the Parisian society participated in these sessions.

What were the planchettes?

They were a kind of board with some wheels underneath and a pen inserted into the front. Participants put their hands on it. Thus they obtained movements that would form words and phrases. At first this was how they communicated with the spirits.

Medium
The phenomena happened because of mediums. Initially the spirits used the movements of the tables to communicate. Then they used a board with wheels on which was placed a pen in the middle, and with the hand of the medium, the automatic writing occurred.

Allan Kardec
He was a very respected teacher with extensive knowledge in various sciences. He was surprised at the level of responses received from the "turning tables".

Did Allan Kardec talk with the "tables"?

Yes, in 1854. Allan Kardec was invited by a friend, Mr. Fortier, to watch the movement of the tables that happened in his house. Allan Kardec, as a researcher, participates in meetings of "turning tables". He observes and notes that they actually moved.

After several meetings, Allan Kardec asks: "How can a table think without a brain and feel without having nerves?" And the table replies: "It is not the table that responds, but the souls of people who had lived on earth that uses the table to communicate."

From the phenomena of "turning tables", Allan Kardec started his serious research regarding communications with the spirits.

Allan Kardec (1804 -1869)

Allan Kardec was an educator, writer and French translator. He lived between the years 1804 and 1869, at the time of Napoleon Bonaparte. He was well known and respected because he had been a student and disciple of Johann Heinrich Pestalozzi, one of the greatest teachers in Europe. In Paris he had contact with various mediums and researched on communication with spirits. He realized that there was a spiritual world consisted of intelligent beings, invisible to our eyes. These beings were spirits. They explained that there was life after death that the important thing is to do good, to practice charity, and that we will live as many times as necessary to become beings of light. Allan Kardec gathered this set of ideas and codified them in several books. He coined the word Spiritism and because of that he became known as the 'Codifier of Spiritism'.

What was the mission of Allan Kardec?

He gives birth to Spiritism, a set of teachings that demonstrates that we are immortal beings who are evolving as spirits for thousands of years until we get to the condition of pure spirits by our own efforts. With this Spiritism answers the perennial questions of humankind: Who are we? Where did we come from? Where are we going?

Personal information:
Name:
Hippolyte-Léon Denizard Rivail - Allan Kardec
Birth:
October 3rd, 1804 in the city of Lyon, France.
Occupation:
Teacher, writer and translator.
Death:
March 31st, 1869, at 64.
Highlight:
"Codifier of Spiritism."

At age 11, Kardec went to study in Switzerland, at the Institute of Education of Yverdon, which was the best school at his time. He was a student of the famous teacher Johann Heinrich Pestalozzi, and he became his disciple and collaborator.

Pestalozzi taught his students that the most important thing in school was not only to receive ordinary education, but also moral education, made up by spiritual values. This would transform human beings in righteous beings.

How did the name Allan Kardec come about?

Professor Hippolyte Léon Denizard Rivail was known by his publications on arithmetic, geometry and translations. At the suggestion of the Spirits, he decided to use the pseudonym Allan Kardec to differentiate the spiritual work from his previously published books.

Allan Kardec is the name that he had in a previous life in France, when he was a druid priest. The druids were a kind of wise monks "Celtic" who lived thousands of years ago in Europe.

Image of the Bookstore Dentu in Paris. The place where "The Spirits' Book" (1857), which is the main work published by Allan Kardec, containing 1018 questions to the Superior Spirits, was released.

What was the work of Allan Kardec?

Allan Kardec wrote several books. The main ones are: "The Spirits' Book", a book that contains 1018 questions to the spirits. After was "The Mediums' Book", "The Gospel According to Spiritism", "Heaven and Hell" and "Genesis".

In the year 1832, he married the teacher Amélie Gabrielle Boudet and founded with her in Paris, an educational school similar to the one of Yverdon.

Père-Lachaise Cemetery (Paris, France)

The dolmen (tomb) of Allan Kardec has Celtic style architecture. Père-Lachaise is the most important cemetery in Paris.

God

Spirits inform us that the harmony that regulates the universe, from atoms to galaxies, has an origin, an initial cause that generated it. All things, forms of life and planets obey the perfect laws and, thereby revealing the existence of an intelligent power. This intelligent Power is God.

In short, the spiritual beings tell us that God is the Supreme Intelligence, the first cause of all things. Therefore, to measure the intelligence of God, just remember the proverb that dictates, 'The worker is known by his or her work.' In that case, to see the work, just look at the Cosmo, the micro-universe, from molecules that are in our hands to the planet we inhabit. So we find out the level of the author's intelligence.

Since ancient times, human beings felt within themselves the existence of God, worshiping nature through rituals, ceremonies and primitive chanting.

Name:
God
Concept:
Supreme Intelligence, the first cause of all things.
Holy Books:
• Bhagavad Gita - Hindus;
• Tipitaka - Buddhists;
• Talmud – Jewish people;
• Bible - Christians;
• Koran – Islamic people.

Humans are not yet able to understand the essential nature of God. Earlier, the idea of God was very simple. Humans attributed to God their own imperfections. So God felt anger, jealousy, He liked a people and hated other, He was violent, etc. As humans evolved, they acquired new values, according to their reason and thus having a better understanding of God.

Where can the proof of God's existence be found?

In a premise that is applied in science: there is no effect without a cause. Investigate the cause of anything that is not the work of human beings and reason shall provide the answer.

How is the nature of God?
The inferiority of human faculties makes it impossible for human beings to fully grasp the essential nature of God. But they can rather have some idea of the attributes of God, which are always in the highest degree. God must possess all these qualities in the supreme degree because if one of them were short or not possessed to an infinite degree, the Creator would not be superior to everything, and thus would not be God.

Attributes of God

Eternal

Infinite

Unchangeable

Immaterial

Unique

All-powerful, Supremely just and good

Does God really exist?

To believe in God, simply observe the works of creation. The universe exists, therefore there is a cause. Doubting the existence of God would be to deny that every effect has a cause, and to presuppose the idea that something could be created from nothing.

At all times, the idea of God was diverse in all societies and existing groups. This is so since the primitive people, when beliefs came from the ancient tribes to modern religions of today's civilization.

Where is written the law of God?

Is it written in a holy book, at some parchment or grave?
No. The spirits replied that it is written in our conscience.
Thus, all humans have within themselves God's law.

15

Spiritist Hierarchy

There are varying degrees of Spirits according to the level of purification that they have attained. If we consider the general characteristics of spirits, we may reduce them to three principal orders. The pure spirits are those who have reached perfection. Those who have reached the middle level are the Good Spirits. And at the bottom of the scale we have the imperfect spirits.

What is free will?

It is the ability the Spirits have to decide whether to do good or evil. All spirits have been created without knowledge of God's laws, to the extent that they evolve over thousands of years, they acquire awareness of themselves and can better choose to do good. Those who do good become pure spirits faster.

Name:
Spiritist Hierarchy
Concept:
Different orders of spirits according to the degree of perfection achieved.
Orders:
1. Pure spirits;
2. Good spirits;
3. Imperfect spirits;
Note:
There are no angels or demons, there are only spirits who do good and those who still have no knowledge of the light.

Why God did not create us already perfect?
Because there would be no merit to enjoy the benefits of being pure spirits. The principle of merit consists of, "to each according to one's works". Therein we see God's justice and wisdom.

God created all Spirits the same, simple and ignorant, that is to say without wisdom. But God has given them the tools to become pure spirits.

Are there demons?

No, if we understand that they are beings created by God to do evil. However, there are evil spirits who still do not practice good. The word demon means genius and was used in Greece under the name daemon, for both good and evil spiritual beings. So all the people had at their side, *daemons* or demons.

No, if we think they are beings that God created good. However, there are spirits who for thousands of years, have been striving to be good, working to be more loving and wise. When Spirits come to this level of goodness and wisdom, we might as well call them "angels". In fact all of us some day will become "angels", and this will depend on our dedication and our free will.

Spirit hierarchy

They are superior in intelligence, wisdom, and love.

Pure Spirits

1st Pure Spirits
Ministers of God

They are spirits who do good, but have not yet become pure.

Good Spirits

2nd Superior Spirits
Science + wisdom + kindness
3rd Scholarly Spirits
knowledge + good judgment
4th Wise Spirits
scientific knowledge
5th Benevolent Spirits
kindness + limited knowledge

They do evil, are proud, selfish, evil and aggressive.

Imperfect Spirits

6th Boisterous and Disruptive Spirits
physical effect
7th Neutral spirits
neither good nor bad
8th False Scholars
knowledge + pride
9th Frivolous Spirits
ignorance + malice
10th Impure Spirits
propensity to evil

The improvement of the Spirits

Spirits can be compared to children. The rebellious and aggressive ones repeat the same school year, having to go through all the tests again. The more docile and hardworking ones go from one grade to another and are deserving of new challenges.

Perispirit

The human being is composed of three bodies. The spirit, the physical body and an intermediate body. This intermediate body is called perispirit. It's a "semi-material" envelope that serves as a 'mold' to the physical body, as if it was the body of the Spirit. Spirits, with their perispirits, can do many things, for example, they can assume the appearance they want. Emmanuel, Chico Xavier's mentor took the appearance of one of his earlier incarnations when he lived in Rome two thousand years ago.

What is the purpose of the perispirit?

It serves mainly for the Spirit to use the physical body. When someone says that they saw a spirit, what they actually saw was the perispirit. Another function of the perispirit is to allow the spirits to contact the mediums, perispirit to perispirit; this is how mediumistic communication occurs. In the perispirit's brain is stored the memories of past lives.

It is in the perispirit that the spirits 'keep' the appearance of their last incarnation.

The perispirit is so subtle that allows spirits to pass through walls, doors, etc.

1st Spirit

This is where lies the intelligence and the consciousness of being.

Allan Kardec says that the perispirit is a byproduct of the universal fluid of each planet.
The more evolved spirits have the subtlest perispirit. In the pure spirits, the perispirit is so ethereal that it does not seem to exist. The perispirit of the imperfect spirits is very dense and heavy.

What can the perispirit do?

Spirits can emit light by their very thought. This is how they, when evolved, radiate light. They can also absorb some physical energy, and the feeling of being temporarily incarnated. Spirits addicted to alcohol and drugs, for example, absorb fluids from incarnate people.

Name: Perispirit
Concept: 'Semi-material' envelope of the Spirit.
Main Function: Enables the union of spirit and physical body.

2nd Perispirit

Body made of a "semi-material" substance. It envelops the Spirit and unites the soul to the physical body.

The centers of force or 'chakras' They are the perispirit's energy centers. They are found in the regions corresponding to the body plexuses. The seven "chakras" are: crown, frontal, throat, heart, gastric, splenic and root or "kundalini".

3rd Physical Body

It is the material body. It has life thanks to the vital principle, equal to that of animals and plants.

19

Spiritual Influence

Spirits are by our side and can see everything we do. They say that they influence our thoughts, our actions, and they do it constantly, all the time. They can also read our thoughts and often suggest ideas to us. Usually when we have a thought, the first that comes to mind is ours, the second is that of the Spirits. When we are engaged in any activity and a thought, a song or a joke comes to mind, we may suspect that this idea was suggested by some spirit.

How can we tell if a thought comes from a good or an evil spirit?

Good spirits advise only for good. We ourselves have to discern case by case.

Name:
Spiritual Influence
Note:
The influence of Spirits upon our thoughts and acts is greater than we suppose, for very frequently it is they who guide us.

Imperfect spirits attach themselves to humans to deviate them from good. They encourage them to vices and passions without limits. But humans always have freedom to either listen and follow them, or to change their lives.

When the physical body dies, the spirits are free and return to the spiritual world or the world of spirits.

Why do imperfect spirits tempt us to wrongdoing?

To make us suffer like they do. This does not lessen their personal suffering, but they do this out of jealousy of those who are happier than themselves.

There are neither angels nor demons. There are only spirits, who are intelligent, who constitute humanity and populate the different planets.

When we say that the reason for our misfortunes is bad luck, in reality we are the ones to blame for not listening to the warnings of the good spirits.

21

Dreams

Dreams are memories that people have of the spirit world when they leave their physical bodies while sleeping. At the time of sleep, spirits with their perispirits partially move away from the body that rests. They come in contact with other spirits and have experiences in the spiritual world.

Spiritual World
During sleep, the Spirit visits the spiritual world, which is the world the Spirit will go after death.

Can we visit someone when we are sleeping?

Yes. When we leave the body we can visit those we wish to meet. We can also meet with loved ones who have disincarnated.

Fluids of the Perispirit
Several fluids maintain the perispirit united to the body during sleep. These ties are only severed when we die.

Spirit and Perispirit
Spirit and perispirit remain outside the physical body while it rests.

The physical body
Rests while the spirit is out.

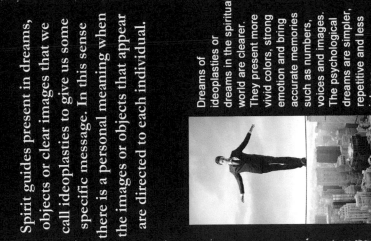

Do dreams have meaning?

Spirit guides present in dreams, objects or clear images that we call ideoplasties to give us some specific message. In this sense there is a personal meaning when the images or objects that appear are directed to each individual.

Dreams of ideoplasties or dreams in the spiritual world are clearer. They present more vivid colors, strong emotion and bring accurate memories such as numbers, voices and images. The psychological dreams are simpler, repetitive and less intense.

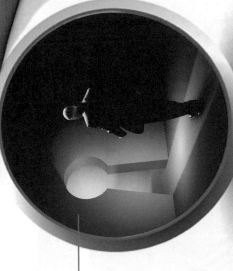

Can we see the future in dreams?

Yes. During the dreams, spirits are free from the physical body and can go to distant places in the hereafter. They can have visions of the past, of other lives, and can see some events that will still occur.

We do not remember our dreams

The dream is the memory of what the Spirit saw during sleep, but we do not always remember it. This is because our spiritual faculties are not yet well developed and because the physical body blocks the impressions received by the spirit during sleep.

We should not be afraid of death, because every day, in a way, we die.

Oftentimes we keep the remembrances that the Spirit has of the experiences lived in the spiritual world during sleep. But sometimes, these memories are mixed with psychological dreams, that is to say, those that are caused by our worries of everyday life.

Name:
Dream
Concept:
The dream is the memory of what the Spirit has seen during sleep.

Mediumship

It is a faculty that enables communication of people with spirits. This faculty is present in thousands of people, regardless of religion, social class, level of education or morals. Mediumship is divided into two major groups: those that produce physical effects, and those who produce intellectual effects.

Mediumship of Physical Effects

Mediums with this faculty are used by the Spirits to provoke various physical movements, such as carrying objects, manipulate perfumes, make raps, lift tables, including making spirits visible. They may even perform healings and surgeries. These mediums are very rare nowadays.

Healing mediums: those who have the power to heal or relieve the pain of patients.

Levitation of a table in a mediumship meeting.

Materialization of the Spirit Katie King next to the researcher Sir William Crookes.

Spirit materialized through the ectoplasm coming out of the medium's mouth Antônio Alves Feitosa that formed the apparition of sister Josefa.

The medium Chico Xavier during a materialization of spirits in the city of Uberaba in 1965.

Mediumship with Jesus
It is mediumship when practiced correctly, following the guidelines of the Gospel, with balance and spiritist study and when put to the service of good.

Mediumship of Intellectual Effects

Mediums with this faculty are those who receive intelligent communications from spirits. They can be speakers, psychographers, hearing mediums, painters, etc. With this mediumship one can learn more about the spiritual world.

Through psychophony or trance, spirits can communicate using the incarnate's vocal organs, to deliver an audible message to all those present.

Painter mediums perform paintings of the most celebrated artists with amazing speed and with the painter's style.

The mediums of psychography have the ability to write while under the influence of spirits.

The writing mediums or psychographers are the most common ones. Of all the forms of communication, psychography is the simplest, the most convenient, and, especially, the most complete.

Intuitive mediumship

There is an inner voice that speaks to the heart. This voice is from the good spirits. If we make an effort to listen to that inner voice that constantly talks to us, we will come eventually to hear our guardian angel who protects us from above.

What is Ectoplasm?

It is a substance that emanates from the body of the medium of physical effect. Through this substance spirits materialize.

Spirits use the ectoplasm that they draw from the mediums' body orifices to be able to materialize. Hereby they become visible and usually present themselves with the appearance of their last incarnation.

Name:
Mediumship

Types of mediumship:
Mediums of physical effects and mediums of intellectual effects.

Other names:
Gift, charisma, talent, faculties, etc.

Mediums

Everyone is a medium. Some, however, only lightly feel the influence of spirits, but others can see them, hear them and write what they dictate. Those who serve as a bridge between the spirits and people, more ostensibly, are considered to be mediums.

If spirits can communicate, that means they always have done that. This finding can be proven throughout history. There have always been people who had the power to see the invisible world and to receive messages: the mediums. In all cultures and religions, they were called many names: pythoness, oracles, prophets, psychics, etc.

When Jesus spoke of mediumship he said to the disciples: "Heal the sick, raise the dead, cleanse those who have leprosy, drive out demons. Freely you have received; freely give." (Mathews, 10:8), Jesus implied that mediumship should be free, because no one should charge for what one have received for free.

Why did Moses prohibit mediumship?

He forbade the Jewish people to communicate with the spirits, because they were misusing mediumship.

At that time, the Jews were freed from slavery in Egypt, and for having lived many centuries in the country, they acquired various habits, such as the use of mediumship for personal gains. Spiritism has demonstrated that the spiritual purpose of mediumship is to comfort and to teach.

Name:
Medium
Source:
From the Latin - medium
Types of Mediums:
Mediums of physical effects and mediums of intellectual effects.
Other names:
pythoness, hierophants, geniuses, prophets, sensitive, psychic, etc.

The mediums receive the spirits' message through the pineal gland, which is located in the center of the brain, at eye level.

The communicant Spirit sends the thought to the medium.

What is the pineal gland?

The Spirit André Luiz, through the automatic writing of Chico Xavier, in the book "Missionaries of Light", considers the pineal gland as the gland of spiritual life. This gland is a kind of antenna that pick up the messages from spirits.

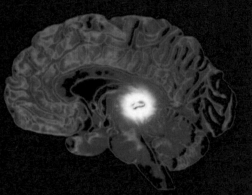

Illustration of the location of the pineal gland.

One of the major problems of mediumship is "obsession". It is the negative influence of a wicked spirit upon the medium.

Who is a good medium?

A good medium is not the one who communicates easily, but one that is pleasing to the good spirits. The medium is always attuned to them and only receives messages from them.

The Mediums' Book (1861):

It is a book written by Allan Kardec. It is the perfect guide for all mediums who truly wish to understand their mediumistic faculties. It also explains how they can use them to comfort people.

Psychography

It's the type of mediumship that allows spirits to communicate in writing. Allan Kardec says that all efforts should be directed towards the mediumship of psychography, because it allows us to establish constant and regular contact with spirits. The faculty of writing is also the easiest mediumship to develop by exercise.

At the time of Allan Kardec, several objects were used to obtain communication with the spirits. At first, some boards and some baskets, with a pen inserted in the center of them, were used to receive the psychography.

Name:
Psychography

Classes:
Mechanical, intuitive and semi-mechanical.

Concept:
Writing of spirits using the medium's hand.

What is the advantage of automatic writing?

By means of psychography, we can more easily identify the spirits' level of evolvement, recognizing whether they are good or bad, wise or ignorant. Through books and psychographic works, we get to know better their way of thinking and the moral teachings they contain, and we also learn about their personality. Precise revelations of the spiritual world are also narrated in psychography.

The Brazilian medium Francisco Cândido Xavier (1910 - 2002) psychographed more than 400 books. He is considered the greatest medium of psychography of all times.

Specular Message written by Léon Denis Spirit through the medium Divaldo Franco in 2004, during the 4th World Spiritist Congress in Paris, France. Léon Denis was a disciple of Allan Kardec.

Divaldo Pereira Franco (1927) is a medium of psychography and psychophony. He has published more than 280 books, through psychography, on Spiritism, under the guidance of spirits, including a series of psychological studies, dictated by his spiritual mentor: Joanna de Angelis.

How many types of writing mediums are there?
The mediums are divided into three classes:

a) Mechanical or Unconscious Mediums
What characterizes the phenomenon in this instance is that the mediums are completely unaware of what they are writing.

b) Semi-Mechanical or Semi-Conscious mediums
Semi-mechanical mediums feel their hand being moved without their willing it to do so, but at the same time they are aware while the words are being formed, of what is being written.

c) Intuitive or Conscious Mediums
A spirit transmits its thought through the medium's soul. The spirit does not act directly upon the hand in order to make it write, but acts upon the soul with which it identifies itself.

Specular Psychography

Specular Psychography is a variant of psychography. The messages received by the medium can only be read with the help of a mirror.

Chico Xavier

(1927 -2002)

Francisco de Paula Cândido Xavier, better known as Chico Xavier, was born in the city of Pedro Leopoldo in 1910 and died in Uberaba in 2002. Chico Xavier was one of the most important disseminators of Spiritism in Brazil and the most active spiritist medium of all times. Through his mediumship he psychographed more than 400 books and sold over 50 million copies. Chico always gave the copyrights of the psychographic works to charities and spiritist organizations. He also received about ten thousand letters from the deceased through psychography and always worked for free. He passed away at age 92, victim of a cardiac arrest.

How did Chico Xavier manage to become the greatest spiritist medium?

The spiritist leader received great honors. In 2000 he was appointed "The most important citizen of Minas Gerais state of the twentieth century" in a contest held by the Brazilian television. In 2006 he was named "The greatest Brazilian in history," in a research promoted by Epoca magazine, and in 2012 he was appointed "The greatest Brazilian of all times" by the public in a TV show.

Emmanuel
Chico was still a young man when he met his spiritual guide Emmanuel. The mentor informed him about his mission to psychograph a series of books and explained to him that he would be required to follow three conditions: "discipline, discipline and discipline." When he was reincarnated at the time of Christ, Emmanuel was the Roman senator Publius Lentulus.

Emmanuel was always adamant in saying to Chico Xavier: "if I ever say anything that is not in accordance with the precepts of Jesus and Kardec, stay with them and forget what I said."

Name:
Francisco de Paula Cândido Xavier, better known as Chico Xavier.
Birth:
April 2nd, 1910, Minas Gerais.
Death:
June 30, 2002, Uberaba, Minas Gerais.
Highlight:
It was the most active spiritist medium of all times.

How many books have Chico Xavier psychographed?

The mediumistic work of Chico Xavier is quite diverse. The Brazilian Spiritist Federation (FEB) alone published more than 18 million copies. The most sought after psychographed book is "Nosso Lar/Our Home". It is a best seller that sold over 2 million copies.

The first book psychographed and published by Chico was " Parnaso de Além Túmulo / Parnassus from beyond the tomb". The work included poems from 56 Brazilian and Portuguese disincarnated poets, and it was received in the years 1931 and 1932. At the time, Chico was only 21 years old.

Interviews in the Pinga-Fogo TV Show
In the 70's Chico participated in TV Shows that reached audience peaks. The main one was "Pinga- Fogo." His participation in the program led him to be known in Brazil, winning admiration and fame.

Chico Xavier was also the most important disseminator of Spiritism in Brazil.

In 1981 he was nominated for the Nobel Peace Prize. About 2 million Brazilian signatures were gathered for his candidacy.

Chico Xavier, the movie (2010)

The life of "Chico Xavier" became a Brazilian film directed by Daniel Filho. It was released in 2010 and it was very successful in Brazil.

Reincarnation

Reincarnation is the return of the Spirit to a new physical body. Thus, the Spirits have many successive existences until their purification. Allan Kardec called it "plurality of existences" and he defined it as the only explanation that corresponds to the idea we form of God's justice toward human beings.

Since immemorial times, reincarnation is part of the knowledge of ancient peoples, initiation centers and religious schools. Belief in reincarnation has its origins in the early days of humanity and its knowledge is the key to understanding the Gospel of Jesus.

Why do we not remember our past lives?

Divine Law does not allow us to remember everything. There is a veil that hides the details of the past so that we can act with greater freedom. If we remembered the past, our lives would nowadays be in torment, because of memories of unfortunate acts that we possibly committed, such as crimes and betrayals.

Reincarnation is one of Spiritism's principles. It is the consequence of two laws: The Law of Divine Justice and the Law of Progress.

Name:
Reincarnation

Concept:
Return of the Spirit to the physical plane.

Other names:
Plurality of existences.
Palingenesis.
Metempsychosis.
Transmigration of souls.
Resurrection in the flesh.
Previous lives.

Brian Weiss PhD
American psychiatrist, Brian Weiss is the author of the book "Many Lives, Many Masters." In the book, he recounts his experiences with Catherine, who was hypnotized by him. She went back to the origin of her problems. She remembered a life when she lived in Egypt in the18th century BCE After experimenting hypnosis with hundreds of patients, Dr. Brian concluded that we all reincarnate.

Can we remember something from previous lives?

Generally yes. We have no exact recollection of what we were, but we have the intuition because our instinctual tendencies are a reminder of the past. Our phobias, traumas, artistic skills, professional vocation, fears, courage, caution, shyness, spontaneity, may have originated in other lives.

Remembering the past could be harmful because it could remind us of former adversaries. Moreover, executioners and victims can be found within our own families and the remembrance would affect our relationship. So forgetting serves us as forgiveness therapy.

How can we prove reincarnation?

The memory of previous lives researched by renowned psychiatrists, is one of the most compelling methods to prove reincarnation. Experiments prove the truth of the past; patients identify places, dates, kinships, names and old facts.

Ian Stevenson PhD (1918-2007)
Psychiatrist and researcher on reincarnation, he gathered more than three thousand cases throughout the world of children who could remember their past lives.

In the Gospel

Jesus taught reincarnation in the Gospel as "resurrection in the flesh." In John 3:1-15 is written in detail, the conversation with Nicodemus:
"Very truly I tell you, no one can see the kingdom of God unless they are born again."

The Earth

Earth is a planet that serves as a dwelling for thousands of incarnate and discarnate spirits. A team of superior spirits, coordinated by Jesus, is in charge of our world.

From time to time, the planet goes through evolutionary stages. Spirits that do not accompany this evolution are taken to a less evolved world. It's like a student who failed one grade in school and need to redo it. This happened to Earth thousands of years ago. When Earth was inhabited by primitive beings, our planet received spirits from another world (Capella) and they formed the civilizations of that time. Currently the Earth is in a transition process. It is ceasing to be a world of "trials and atonements," in which evil prevails in people, to become a world of "regeneration", with a more peaceful humanity.

Formation of living beings
In the beginning all was chaos. Jesus and the spiritual team gradually were placing the land, the air and the water in their respective places.

Name: Earth
Age: 4.54 billion years
Approximate population:
7 billion (incarnates)
15 billion (discarnates)
Stage:
In Transition, from world of "trials and atonements to regeneration.
Races of the Earth:
Yellow and Black
Races of Capella:
Egyptians
Indo-European family
The people of Israel
Castes in India

The Pure Spirits, coordinated by Jesus, brought down a sort of cloud over the Earth that covered the planet. It was like a gelatinous mass from which appeared the first living beings.

Plurality of worlds
All worlds are inhabited by living beings, incarnates and discarnates. To believe that there is only life on our planet is to ignore the Divine Wisdom that does not make anything useless.
All worlds have a destiny.

The transitional worlds
Transitional worlds are worlds particularly destined to spirits who are not reincarnated. These worlds can serve as temporary housing, a kind of resting camps. Planet Earth belonged to this class during its formation thousands of years ago, when there were only volcanoes and lava flowing on its surface.

What is Capella?

It is the brightest star in the constellation Auriga. It is about 42 light-years from Earth. Millions of rebellious spirits were expelled from the planet Capella and welcomed by Jesus in our orb. This happened thousands of years ago.

Who are the exiles of Capella?
They are rebellious spirits, expelled from Capella that reincarnated on Earth. The black and yellow races originate on our planet. The exiles of Capella form four other races: the Arians, the civilization of Egypt, the people of Israel and the castes of India.

Egyptians
It was the Egyptians who have stood out in doing good. Some of them returned to Capella, but many remained with Jesus on Earth.

Indo-European family
They have no religious feeling, as they bring from Capella an intimate revolt. Their greatest virtues lie in their fraternization with the savages of Europe. They are the basis of the white race.

The people of Israel
They are the strongest, more homogeneous, and proud race. They were also monotheist, and Jesus chose them because of their faithfulness and need.

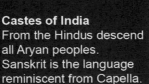

Castes of India
From the Hindus descend all Aryan peoples. Sanskrit is the language reminiscent from Capella.

On the Way to the Light

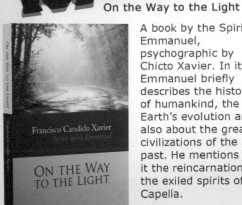

A book by the Spirit Emmanuel, psychographic by Chicto Xavier. In it, Emmanuel briefly describes the history of humankind, the Earth's evolution and also about the great civilizations of the past. He mentions in it the reincarnation of the exiled spirits of Capella.

Apparition of Human Beings
Humans appeared in many places and at different times. On Earth, there were two main races: the black and yellow ones; adapted to the climate, life and customs.

Prayer

Prayer is the way that people have to attract help, guidance and comfort from the good spirits. They come to support us in our good decisions and inspire us good thoughts.

Spirits always say:

"Words are worth nothing, the thought is everything." Thus, each must pray with sincerity and according to one's beliefs. A good thought is worth much more than saying a prayer with elaborate words and no feelings.

Collective prayer

Collective prayer becomes more effective when all who pray unite their hearts, to a single thought and with a single purpose.

Can we pray for others?

Yes. When we pray for others, we do this because of a desire to do good.

Name:
Prayer
Source:
Prayers (Latin prayers, plural of prex, "prayer")
Concept:
Thought directed to attract the help of good spirits.
Types of spiritist prayers:
I - General Prayers
II - Prayers for yourself
III - Prayers for others
IV - Prayers for the dead
V - Prayers for the sick and obsessed

Jesus teaches us that we can make requests during prayers. But it would be illogical if such requests were only about material things, as Providence knows what is best for us. What we should ask is for courage, patience and resignation.

In prayer, every word must have a sense and spark an idea, that is, it must lead us to reflect.

How should we pray?
All prayers are good when made with love and emotion. They should be clear, simple and concise.

1. Clear
It is very important to be clear, easy to understand. Prayers that are pronounced in unknown languages, for example, may have no value.

2. Simple
Prayer should be simple, without complicated words or created phrases.

3. Concise
Each word should make us reflect on what is thought or spoken.

During the prayer we may ask the good spirits to inspire us with good ideas to help us solve our difficulties.

Do powerful prayers exist?
No. The spirits claim that there is no magic formula or powerful prayers. The purpose of prayer is to raise our souls. Therefore, the different ways they are conducted make no difference.

Spirits teach some prayers to help those who find it difficult to express their ideas, because there are people who, if they do not read or repeat a prayer, they believe that they did not pray.

Jesus

Jesus is the spirit responsible for the creation of our planet. When he incarnated on Earth, he taught us the supreme law of unconditional love:
"Love your neighbor, including the enemies."
The existence of Jesus was an example of doing good, forgiveness of sins, and charity toward all, so his life serves us to follow as model. His teachings of humility and love were recorded in the Gospels and are moral guidelines for us. Jesus is recognized as a model and guide for humanity. His life is the way to know the truth.

Is Jesus the ruler of the planet?

Yes. He coordinates the team of angelic spirits responsible for Earth's harmony and evolution.

He is part of the community of divine spirits, coordinators of life in all planets.

Socrates
He was the greatest of all Greek philosophers of antiquity.
Socrates was sent by Christ 350 years before his coming to earth to teach many moral lessons, preparing the way for Christianity's message. The ideas of God, the immortality of the soul, life after death, of the importance of doing good, the responsibility for our actions, are also principles of Spiritism.

Name:
Jesus of Nazareth
Born: 8-4? BCE
Place:
Belem - Roman province of Judea.
Death:
29-36? A.D.
Location:
Jerusalem - Judea.
Occupation on Earth:
Carpenter and rabbi.
Spiritual Occupation:
Earth's Coordinator.

Jesus announced the coming of the Consoler, the Spirit of Truth, who would teach all spiritual truths and to remind us of what he had said.

Spiritism is the promised Consoler. It came to accomplish what Jesus said: knowledge of the spiritual world, leading human beings to know who they are, from where did they come from, and to where they will go. It comes to remind us of Christ's message in all its purity.

What did Jesus teach?

Jesus' teachings are in the Gospels. We highlight the "Sermon on the Mount." They are behavioral lessons that dictate the principles that lead to righteousness, such as humility, compassion, gentleness, peace, fairness and purity of heart. They can be considered as a summary of the teachings regarding the access to the spiritual world.

Beatitudes

1. Blessed are the poor in spirit,
2. Blessed are those who mourn,
3. Blessed are the meek,
4. Blessed are those who hunger and thirst for righteousness,
5. Blessed are the merciful,
6. Blessed are the pure in heart,
7. Blessed are the peacemakers,
8. Blessed are those who are persecuted because of righteousness,
9. Blessed are you when people insult you, persecute you and falsely say all kinds of evil against you because of me.

Has Jesus performed miracles?

The greatest miracle that Jesus performed was the revolution that his teachings of love and forgiveness caused in humans. This message is able to change them, making them become good beings, thus transforming the world.

The spiritist moral is based on the Gospel of Jesus, which is the example of moral conduct to be followed.

The Gospel According to Spiritism (1864)

This book helps us to understand the lessons of Jesus and to apply them on a daily basis. This book teaches Christianity, including comments from Allan Kardec and the Superior Spirits on the main messages of Jesus.

Spiritist Timeline

The Exiled People of Capella

There is a community of pure spirits, directors of planets, and Jesus is one of its divine members.
These spirits have met twice:

Pure Spirits modify the perispirit of primitive beings, perfecting the human races.

Indo-European family
The Arians, from which most white people descend. These groups lack religious affection and occupy the regions of present-day Europe.

First meeting
It happened when the planet Earth was detaching from the Sun's Nebula, to plan the start of material life.

The black and yellow race originated on the planet.

Christ receives four groups of exiled rebel spirits from an orb of Capella star.
These four groups will form the basis of future civilizations.

Castes of India
The Hindus, from which all Aryan peoples descend. They constituted castes and started Hinduism, and later on Buddhism.

30 A.D. Israel
The Second Revelation
Jesus teaches the Gospel, the Beatitudes and brings the Law of Love on Earth.

34 A.D. Damascus, Syria
Paul converted to Christianity and begins spreading the doctrine in the West.

The people of Israel
The Hebrews were the strongest race and more homogeneous, monotheistic and proud.

1,280 B.C.E Mount Sinai, Egypt
The First Revelation
Moses receives "The 10 Commandments".

Second meeting
It was held to decide the coming of Jesus to Earth, in order to teach humanity the lesson of his Gospel of unconditional love.

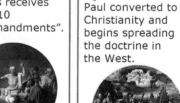

24,000 BCE Middle East
Christ gathered the exiled in Iran's plateau, to guide them before their reincarnation on Earth.

The Egyptian civilization
Egyptians are the most evolved people of Capella.

450 B.C.E Athens, Greece
Socrates disseminates the philosophical teachings, starting the path to Christianity.

312 A.D. Rome, Italy
Emperor Constantine becomes Christian. Years later Christianity becomes the official religion of the Roman Empire.

4.6 billion years	4000 BCE	476 A.D.
PREHISTORY	OLD AGE	MIDDLE AGE

1 to 4 million years B.C.E

Year 0

HUMANS APPEARS ON EARTH

SPIRITUAL MATURITY OF PLANET EARTH

**1500
United States**
Christ determines America to be the brain of the new civilization and culture.

**1848
Hydesville, United States**
Phenomena of raps happen in the house of the Fox sisters. It represents the starting point of Spiritism.

**1850
France**
The turning tables phenomena become popular in French society.

Dates of the Three Western Revelations:

**1280 BCE
First Revelation**
Mount Sinai, Egypt (Moses)

**30 A.D.
Second Revelation**
Israel (Jesus)

**1857
Third Revelation**
Paris, France (Spiritism)

**1500
Brazil**
Christ entrusts to Angel Ismael the Brazilian territory, destined to become the "Heart of the World and Homeland of the Gospel."

**1815
Yverdon**
Pestalozzi, the great Swiss pedagogue, became a teacher of the young Hippolyte Denizard, later known as Allan Kardec.

**1857
Paris, France
The Third Revelation**
Allan Kardec publishes "The Spirits' Book" and Spiritism begins.

**1884
Rio de Janeiro (RJ)**
Brazilian Spiritist Federation (FEB) is founded by Augusto Elias da Silva.

**1927
Feira de Santana (BA)**
The medium and speaker Divaldo Franco reincarnates. He dedicated his life to the dissemination of Spiritism in the world.

**1800
Europe**
Christ summons spiritual guides from around the world to start the Third Revelation.

**1831
Riacho do Sangue**
Bezerra de Menezes reincarnates, "The doctor of the poor" who would implement Spiritism in Brazil.

**1861
Barcelona, Spain**
In the public square are burned 300 spiritist books, the so-called "Auto of Faith in Barcelona."

**1910
Pedro Leopoldo (MG)**
Chico Xavier, the greatest spiritist medium of all times reincarnates. He psychographed over 400 spiritist books.

**1992
Madrid, Spain.**
International Spiritist Council is founded, institution resulting from the meeting of spiritist organizations in the world.

1453 A.D.	1789 A.D.	today
MODERN AGE	CONTEMPORARY AGE	

(Date unknown)

THIRD MEETING OF PURE SPIRITS
TO DESIGNATE EARTH'S FUTURE AS A WORLD OF REGENERATION

Spiritist Geographic Map

Paris - 1857
Third Revelation
Allan Kardec publishes "The Spirits' Book" and Spiritism begins.

Madrid - 1992
The International Spiritist Council, institution resulting from the meeting of spirit entities in the world is founded.

Hydesville - 1848
Phenomena of rappings occur in the home of the Fox Sisters. Its Spiritism's starting point.

Riacho do Sangue - 1831
Bezerra de Menezes, "The doctor of the poor" reincarnates. He implemented Spiritism in Brazil.

Feira de Santana - 1927
The medium and speaker Divaldo Franco reincarnates. He dedicated his life to the dissemination of Spiritism in the world.

United States - 1500
Christ assigns America to be the brain of the new civilization and culture.

Brazil - 1500
Christ assigns Brazil to angel Ishmael. Brazil is destined to be the "Heart of the World and the Homeland of the Gospel."

The Three Western Revelations:

First Revelation
1280 BCE
Mount Sinai, Egypt
(Moses)

Second Revelation
30 A.D.
Israel (Jesus)

Third Revelation
1857 Paris, France
(Spiritism)

Pedro Leopoldo (MG) - 1910
Chico Xavier, the greatest spiritist medium of all times reincarnates. He psychographed over 400 spiritist books.

Rio de Janeiro - 1884
Brazilian Spiritist Federation (FEB) is founded by Augusto Elias da Silva.

Europe - 1800
Christ summons spiritual guides from around the world to start the Third Revelation.

France - 1850
The phenomena of the turning tables become popular in French society.

Yverdon - 1815
Pestalozzi, the great Swiss pedagogue, became a teacher of the young Hippolyte Denizard, later known as Allan Kardec.

Greece - 450 B.C.E
Socrates disseminates the philosophical teachings, starting the path to Christianity.

Asia
The yellow race originated on the planet.

Damascus - 34 A.D.
Paul converted to Christianity and begins spreading the doctrine in the West.

Indo-European family
The Arians, from which most white people descend. These group lack religious affection and occupy the regions of present-day Europe.

24,000 BCE - Middle East
Christ gathered the exiled in Iran's plateau, to guide them before their reincarnation on Earth.

Barcelona- 1861
In a public square, 300 spiritist books are burned, in the so-called "Auto of Faith in Barcelona."

Rome - 312
Emperor Constantine makes Christianity the official religion of the Roman Empire.

The Egyptian civilization
Egyptians are the most evolved people of Capella. They lived in this region.

The people of Israel
The Hebrews were the strongest race and more homogeneous, monotheistic and proud.

Castes of India
The Hindus, from which all Aryan peoples descend. They constituted castes and began Hinduism, and later on Buddhism.

Egypt - 1280 B.C.E
The First Revelation
Moses receives "The 10 Commandments" on Mount Sinai.

Israel – A.D. 30.
The Second Revelation
Jesus teaches the Gospel, the Beatitudes and brings the Law of Love on Earth.

The Exiled People of Capella
The four spiritual groups depart from the Middle East region (Iran) and move to four geographic Regions.

- Indo-European family
- Castes of India
- The Egyptian civilization
- The people of Israel

Africa
The black race originated on the planet.

43

More information about the author:

www.luishu.com

Made in the USA
Columbia, SC
20 January 2018